Dear Parent,

In <u>What Is Gravity?</u> your child will learn that gravity is a force that keeps things in place. Monkey uses an apple to show Christopher and his friends how gravity works. Then it's off to a ball game to learn what gravity does to a baseball. Grab your bat and ball, peanuts and popcorn, and head for the park.

Sincerely,

Rita D. Gould

Managing Editor

FAMILY FUN

- Demonstrate how gravity works. Have your child stand on a chair or bench and drop a bean bag (a heavy object) to the floor. Have your child drop the bean bag and a pencil (a light object) at the same time. Help your child understand that both hit the floor at the same time.

- Some lightweight objects catch air currents as they fall, slowing down the fall. Have your child stand on a chair and drop a bean bag and a sheet of paper at the same time. Help your child understand why the paper falls more slowly than the bean bag.

READ MORE ABOUT IT

- *Why Does It Fly?*
- *What Is a Space Shuttle?*
- *What Is a Wave?*

This book is a presentation of Weekly Reader
Books. Weekly Reader Books offers book
clubs for children from preschool through high
school. For further information write to:
WEEKLY READER BOOKS, 4343 Equity Drive,
Columbus, Ohio 43228

This edition is published by arrangement
with Checkerboard Press.

Weekly Reader is a federally registered trademark
of Field Publications.

WEEKLY READER BOOKS presents

What Is Gravity?

A **Just Ask**™ Book

Hi, my name is Christopher!

by Chris Arvetis
and Carole Palmer

illustrated by
Vernon McKissack

FIELD PUBLICATIONS
MIDDLETOWN, CT.

It's a very hard thing
to explain.
But I'll try.
Let's start with the apple.

This is interesting!

When I drop the apple,
it falls to the ground.
Watch it fall.

Look out,
Christopher!

When I jump off this rock,
I fall to the ground.
You try it, too.

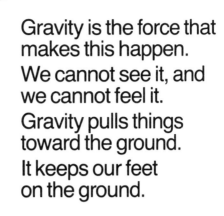

Gravity is the force that
makes this happen.
We cannot see it, and
we cannot feel it.
Gravity pulls things
toward the ground.
It keeps our feet
on the ground.

Just imagine if we lived in a place where there was no gravity.

Look at these pictures.

They show what it would be like.

See our friends floating in the air.

Everything would float in the air.
Look at the chair and table.
They float just like the animals.

Gravity on the earth keeps us on the ground.
A scientist—
Isaac Newton—
studied about gravity.
He told us many things about gravity.

Now, if we look at the apple on the ground, it will never start to move by itself. Gravity holds it in place. It will never move unless someone or something makes it.

We can see this if we look at a ball game.
The ball keeps on moving as long as the players are hitting it back and forth.

Once the ball stops, someone
or something has to make
it move.

Or gravity will hold the ball
right where it is.

Gravity holds you on the ground and keeps things in place around you.
It is a part of our world on earth.